Alley of Dreams

Poems by

Anne Britting Oleson

Clare Songbirds Publishing House Chapbook Series
ISBN 978-1-947653-18-4
Clare Songbirds Publishing House
Alley of Dreams © 2018 Anne Britting Oleson
All Rights Reserved. Clare Songbirds Publishing House retains right to reprint.
Permission to reprint individual poems must be obtained from the author who owns the copyright.

Printed in the United States of America
FIRST EDITION

Clare Songbirds Publishing House Mission Statement:
Clare Songbirds Publishing House was established to provide a print forum for the creation of limited edition, fine art from poets and writers, both established and emerging. We strive to reignite and continue a tradition of quality, accessible literary arts to the national and international community of writers, and readers. Chapbook manuscripts are carefully chosen for their ability to propel the expansion of art and ideas in literary form. We provide an accessible way to promote the art of words in order to resonate with, and impact, readers not yet familiar with the siren song of poets and writers. Clare Songbirds Publishing House espouses a singular cultural development where poetry creates community and becomes commonplace in public places.

140 Cottage Street
Auburn, New York 13021
www.ClareSongbirdspub.com

Contents

Ruelle des Rêves	7
My Love Lives Behind a Blue Door	8
Ball	9
Snow Ghosts	10
Dover Road	11
The Clank of Bells in the Roadway	12
The Wind in the Chimney	13
Ghosts at the Edge of Sleep	14
Shade	15
Haunt	16
Nocturne	17
December Dusk	18
Birch	19
The Border	20
Imbolc	21
The Dead are Real	22
Handwriting	23
My Father did not Drown When He Was Twelve	24
Haunting	25
Third Horse	26
No Shadows	27
Ghosts	28
Lamp	29
Looking Back Up the Hospital Drive	31

Some of these poems have appeared in the following publications, sometimes in different forms:

"Ruelle des Rêves" - *A New Ulster*
"Ball" - *Lavender Wolves Literary Journal*
"Dover Road" - *Apple Valley Review*
"Ghosts at the Edge of Sleep" - *Gravel: a Literary Journal*
"Nocturne" - *Window-Lit Mag*
"Birch" - *East Coast Literary Review*
"The Dead are Real" - *The MacGuffin ("The Dead are Real")*
"My Father Did not Drown when he was Twelve" - *Heartbeat*
"Haunting" - *Epicentre Magazine*
"Third Horse" - *Fox Cry Review*
"Ghosts" - *Aardvark Press*
"The Border" - *Clementine Poetry Journal*
"Looking Back Up the Hospital Drive" - *Valparaiso Poetry Review*
"Looking Back Up the Hospital Drive" also appeared in *The Church of St. Materiana* (Moon Pie Press, 2007).

For Julia and Roger, who know how much I love ruinous things;

And for John Ford, for dancing in the haunted ballroom

~Anne Britting Oleson

Ruelle des Rêves

I was searching for a door.
It might have been yours.
The number, on a scrap of paper,
ran in blue rivulets—
from the rain, or
perhaps from tears.

I know it was late.
Far away, a clock rang the hour.
Overhead, between the roofs,
a sliver of sky hung, unstarred.

Only a single window,
high above the lane, was lit.
As I stood rooted,
that light, too, went out.

A cold wind skittered
a newspaper along the cobbles,
raised goosebumps
on my bare arms.
I turned at the sound
of measured footsteps,
but no one was there.

I thought: *I've been here before.*
I thought: *I cannot go on.*
I might have leaned against
the weeping stone wall, despairing.
Perhaps I wondered why,
still, you did not come.

Alley of Dreams

My Love Lives Behind a Blue Door

I do not yet know his name.
My love—for that he is—
walks the lanes at twilight,
his hands clasped behind his back.
He hums softly to himself,
sometimes a happy song, sometimes
melancholy, and yet hopeful;
but always he looks up
into the hushed breathing of leaves
against the evening sky.
I want him to wear a flat cap,
a jacket with leather elbow patches.
I want it to be autumn.
When the sun sets,
he lets himself in
through the cottage's blue door,
touches a match to the fire.
My love—I cannot see his face—
will settle in with a book
and a tumbler of scotch,
but will be distracted from reading
as he imagines, in his turn, me.

Ruelle des Rêves

Ball

Blue-veined, the marble pillars
soar up into the darkness
toward windows which would be
sunbursts if there were sun,
if they were not begrimed
with years of dust and cobwebs.
The smell is earthy with
leftover corsages and cigarettes.
Sound crowds back in from
the foxed mirrors on the walls: strings
and horns from a long-dead orchestra.
You sense them all—the tails,
the organdy gowns—as they swirl past,
the ghostly coquettes smiling
at men who sailed long ago
from this sparkling promise
into disappointed old age and death.
Still, you lift your arms
to your phantom partner,
your footprints in the dust like those
of a drunken man in snow.

(for John Ford)

Snow Ghosts

A bit before dusk.
On a seldom-traveled road,
they leap snow-plowed banks,
swirling across the greyed tar,
arms flailing, mouths stretched and howling,
leaving the faintest tracks:
the blue-cold ectoplasm of winter.

Dover Road

Up the hill from your farmhouse lies
a village which is no longer.
No post office, beams moldering
in cellar holes, general store
long closed, leaving windows
with panes falling out like
rotting teeth. When the east wind
blows off the ocean, piano wires
hum in an abandoned house.

Down here the company falls silent
and draws close around the hearth.
Kitchen lights flicker on at nightfall.
I think I hear those echoes
as the snow falls on someone's lost dream
of a town so long gone from the map
that no one alive remembers
when Dover Road was moved:
even this house has turned its back,
the green-fanned front door
gazing down the fields toward the bay.
The storm howls around us,
ghosts unable to find their way home.

The Clank of Bells in the Roadway

After sundown, the shapeshifters,
darker than the air through which they move,

shuffling beneath occasional lowing,
smell of dung and sweet clover.

They are warp to the weft of our evening:
safe inside around the lamp,

we don't see them until they're gone,
and then we're uncertain they were here at all.

The Wind in the Chimney
for H. M.

The old house breathes, and you do, too,
and I: steadily, easily. The floorboards,
the joists all creak, talking
amongst themselves companionably,
while we maintain a companionable silence:
me with my book, you with the orange,
the sock, the gentle hush
of the darning needle.
In other rooms the children lie sleeping,
the music they dream theirs alone.
A ripple of wind whispers in the chimney,
sighing into the grate where no fire burns.
It is late. I look up
to see you gazing ceilingwards.
When I lay aside the book,
you hold up a pale hand.
Listen, you murmur, *to the night.*
Its voice is soft, like yours.
I am comforted by its feather touch.
Come to bed, I say.

Ghosts at the Edge of Sleep

They are trying not to interrupt my sleep,
the old occupants of the older house,
stepping lightly on the stairs.

One at a time they open doors,
cross ill-fitting floorboards, close
things up again behind.

All this I hear on the edges
of waking, not quite a dream:
I know why they don't leave me alone,

and yet they try not to bother me,
allowing me to go about the business
of nighttime in the house we uneasily share.

Shade

She held the peppermill
in her palm, the pad
of her thumb caressing the grain,
and saw it again in his hand,
felt the warmth
his touch had left.

In the bath, the mirror
over the sink for a moment
gave back his reflection,
his chin half-white
with shaving cream,
the razor poised at his jaw.

The traitorous garden tools
resisted her. The car
turned over sluggishly.
Each part of her life bore
his fingerprints. Each breath
she drew in carried his scent.
The air hummed like
the paired strings of his mandolin.

Though she reminded herself
again and again of
the soft cool feel of his lids
beneath her fingertips as
she had closed his eyes, gently,
she still glanced up every time
at the sound of a footfall,
at the creaking of a door.

Haunt
for T. C.

He hears her footsteps on the back stairs,
her tuneless humming from the kitchen.
How well he knows those little sounds
after all their years of marriage—
the ones she never noticed making,
the whispers of simply crossing
the floors of this thoughtless world.
It's been a week. Then a month. A year.
He knows now not to turn, to look for her,
the tiny spark of hope replaced
by the stinking miasma of hopelessness.
The flash of sunlight on her golden hair,
seen out of the corner of his eye,
is an illusion born of the mixed parentage
of desire and grief. It's been so long.
And yet. When he wakes in tangled sheets
to the sly fingers of another cold dawn,
his arms still full of the shape of her body,
his nose still full of the scent of her skin,
it always comes as a shock, that empty dream.

Nocturne

What wakes you? Could it be
the same thing which woke him,
that man out on the road
in the depths of this winter night,
a black silhouette against the dark?
You sit on the edge of the bed,
listening to the pounding in your ears,
breathing deeply. The man does not know
you watch him. In the regular pulse
of the stoplight at the corner,
you see him lift his chin, gazing
upward toward the slow intent walk
of the stars across the sky.
Hand against the glass,
you want to reach for him, touch
his perfect solitude, join him, even:
in the faintly drifting snow,
in the brief flare of the match
he cups in his curved hands,
leaning his cigarette into the flame
before he tosses the match away,
a brilliant arc burning out
before it reaches the ground,
you are awash in nostalgia
for a moment not yet gone
before the man turns and walks on.

December Dusk

She wipes her breath from the window.
Outside the birches are ghosts
raising their spindly arms;
pale against the dying day,
they wail against the coming of winter.
She draws the ring from her left hand
and peers through it, as through a telescope,
the wrong way, making
the world smaller, tighter.
The sky bleeds into a night
which skirs with the cry
of a lost soul. Bone marrow
feels the oncoming freeze.
She bends stiffly and places
the ring in the ashes on the hearth.
Tonight there will be snow.

Ruelle des Rêves

Birch

They stand, ghosts supplicating
with upraised arms, and she is haunted.

She returns to this birch ring,
called by their inaudible voices.

They are immutable.
She wants to be one of them.

In the fall they drop their yellow cloaks;
she wraps her arms around herself.

Winter licks their white trunks
and she dares not leave tracks.

She learns from the trees
how to remain upright and rooted.

The Border

The wood is haunted.
Dead children play there,
and you hear them laugh,
but not in fun, as
they flit through trees:
girls in floating white dresses,
boys in short pants.
In the background, a cello
in a minor key, bow scraping—
or perhaps it's the wind.
Below, the lonely houses
huddle together, cold and dark,
trying not to attract the attention
of the ghost hound at the ridge.
This pathway is forbidden, foreboding,
and at the crack of a branch,
you whirl, eyes wide, breath harsh,
looking for that one thing
you will not see
over your shoulder.

Imbolc

The dawn frowned with the threat of snow.
And so I rose and dressed,
and went alone to walk by the river,
frozen as it was in midwinter.
The world was silent.
I lowered my head,
chastised by the frigid air.
Across the barren stretch of ice,
trees encased in snow,
the black hulk of a sleeping cottage,
smoke from the chimney
rising up and folding sharply
where it met the low clouds.
The winter birds lay hidden.
Yet further along the bank,
beyond the reeds standing at attention
in the still morning,
tiny tracks in the snow,
a tuft of fur, two red droplets.
Hands in pockets, I looked up
to see what might have me in its sights.

The Dead are Real

The ghosts of the Foggs, my Irish grandmother
called the unseen hands which
slammed the door into the woodshed,
which slapped the shades up
in a room she'd just left moments before.
They knocked flowerpots off window ledges,
disinterred the roots of geraniums.
Things were never where she'd left them—
silverware turned up in the bath tub,
garden tools inside the kerosene stove.
There were hallways in that house
cats refused to enter, laying their ears back;
knockings on doors which made
dogs growl and bare their teeth.
My grandmother learned never
to enter rooms without announcing herself:
she'd never seen any Foggs in the house,
though she'd bought it fifty years before
from the last of them, and she had
no intention of meeting any now.
Practical she was, but impatient: *I just wish
I hadn't bought such a crowded house.*

Handwriting

She finds her mother's cursive,
looping inside the cover
of *Anybody Can Cook,*
setting forth the ingredients
for a paintbrush cleaner,
fighting a left-handed lean
with big circles the way
a 1940's student would learn.

Further into the cookbook,
her older sister's squarer hand
instructs what to do
when there's no square
of baking chocolate
for Christmas cookies:
one tablespoon extra butter
to every four of cocoa.

This makes her surprisingly sad,
the swirls of ink against
the yellowed pages: she'd know
those hands anywhere,
recognizes them over time and distance,
but at the words,
she has to stop, has to think,
and it's futile, because
the words are there, but the voices gone.

My Father Did Not Drown When He Was Twelve

My father did not drown when he was twelve,
when, walking home from a baseball game
with his older brother—who would later
become my Uncle George—all boy-sweat and dust
and torn pants, the two jumped the fence
at the city reservoir and stripped naked
in the darkness beyond streetlights
to leap into a private baptism.

When the coldness closed over his head,
shocking his skin and teeth and brain
to numbness, and he breathed that water
into his protesting lungs, my father did not think
of me or my sisters or brother yet to be born,
did not think of a future other than the one
in the moment before him when his brother
grabbed his arm and guided his hand
to the edge, black against the black night.

And when he hung there, coughing up death,
he did not wonder about how, years later,
after decades of Pall Malls he had yet to smoke,
those same lungs would fail him, hack
for air as he might. No. He did not drown
that night at twelve, but grabbed what hold
he could on life, and looked up, unseeing,
at the vague and impersonal stars.

Haunting

I do not recognize the landscape, but realize,
as one finds the way in dream country:
these are the Smokey Mountains.
I stand at the foot of a path leading upwards,
tunneled by the golds of maple, ash, aspen,
and know that my brother is up there,
around a bend, behind a glacial tumble of stone.
My brother, dead these three years.
I call to him, and his name chokes in my mouth,
the rustling of leaves grows louder,
until the trees are all mocking me
with their derisive laughter.
My brother will not answer, here in the forest.
Something far beyond death keeps him,
beyond the scattering of his ashes
beside the Little Pigeon River.
It's sheer cussedness: he wants something—
he always wants something—and until
I come bearing it, an offering in my hands,
he will not be appeased. If only he would tell me
what I need to do—to say—to know.
I call again. No answer. I wake with the taste
of old tears in my throat. Behind the house,
coyotes cry. They give no answer, either.

Third Horse

They trail across the high ridge,
two, then a third, pale
and riderless, their manes and tails
following on the cold air.
Or perhaps they don't.
Far below, in the shadow of the trees,
you hold yourself still
and wait for them, ears straining
for the insistent thud of hooves,
hard on the winter ground.
Beware the third horse,
the old woman had told you
over the January fire,
for it's the one to watch for,
the one you don't want to see.
If the saddle is empty, she said,
death has dismounted.
Now here you are,
your shadow stretching away,
the quiet air sharp as knives,
the ridge splashed with the red
of the dying day, and you
look again for the horses
which may or may not thunder past.

Ruelle des Rêves

No Shadows

The Travelers say noontime is the most dangerous,
call it the time of no shadows.
Perhaps what they mean is there's no warning—
the angry spirits appear so suddenly,
you never see them come.
No place to hide, either, for you:
no dark corners for concealment.

And somehow, today, standing among
the ruins of this Welsh priory
under a relentless midday sun,
you know what that means:
arches, desecrated hundreds of years ago,
no longer holding vaulted ceilings aloft,
still rage against the lust and avarice
which tore them apart, even as
they march in brilliant disguise
toward the open and haunted Brecons.
The stones in their bed of cut grass murmur darkly,
or perhaps that's the foreboding in your blood.

Ghosts

She slumps against the bridge rail, exhausted.
Past midnight, and fog rises from the water,
gliding silently toward her with clammy hands.

It wants her. She knows it's the only thing
that does. Across the lake, a mile away,
lights should be flickering out, people—

strangers—who haven't driven all this way
with ghosts—are retiring to their beds,
looking forward to sunrise and another day,

if only she could see them. But she sees nothing,
save the night and the fog. She has stopped
only because there's nothing left in the tank—

the road does not end here, it coils away
into the darkness—but she can follow it
no further. Her phantom passenger, a child

with wide eyes and outstretched arms,
is silent now, too. Only the soughing
of a weak wind in the trees, and the murmur

of water passing beneath the bridge,
whispering her name. Whispering it again.

Ruelle des Rêves

Lamp

In the night
I stand on the crest
of the autumn hill
and shout.
A single word.
No echo calls back.
No sound bounces
from hill to hill.
Even the birds,
surprised, grow still.
I wait, listening.
I turn, looking downhill
in every direction.
Again, I shout,
wait, look.
In the dark dome
overhead,
a lone star gives
a pinpoint answer.

Looking Back Up the Hospital Drive

They do not come easy to me, these words
like glass in my mouth, cutting until
I taste blood:

the blood whispering through the chambers
of an enlarged heart, failing
the old woman at the upstairs window.

Is she real, or an old reflection, standing
with an upraised hand, waving
or patting hair into place?

This place with the barred windows, gray
in stone, in hair, in face, in clothing,
all color washed away,

washed away like the ink on a letter
left to suffer the laundry, forgotten
in a pocket, words never sent, never read.

www.ingramcontent.com/pod-product-compliance
Lightning Source LLC
Chambersburg PA
CBHW030203100526
44592CB00009B/421